D0812051

The Phoenix Living Poets

MORE THAN TIME

Poets Published in
The Phoenix Living Poets Series

★

Alexander Baird · Alan Bold
George Mackay Brown
Jennifer Couroucli
Gloria Evans Davies
Patric Dickinson · D. J. Enright
John Fuller · David Gill
J. C. Hall · Molly Holden
John Horder · P. J. Kavanagh
Richard Kell · Laurie Lee
Laurence Lerner
Christopher Levenson
Edward Lowbury · Norman MacCaig
James Merrill · Ruth Miller
Leslie Norris · Robert Pack
Arnold Rattenbury
Adrienne Rich · Jon Silkin
Jon Stallworthy
Gillian Stoneham
Edward Storey · Terence Tiller
Sydney Tremayne
Lotte Zurndorfer

MORE THAN TIME

by

PATRIC DICKINSON

CHATTO AND WINDUS

THE HOGARTH PRESS

1970

Published by
Chatto and Windus Ltd
with The Hogarth Press Ltd
42 William IV Street
London WC 2
*
Clarke, Irwin and Co Ltd
Toronto

ISBN 0 7011 1666 8

Printed in Great Britain at
The Blackmore Press, Gillingham, Dorset
by T. H. Brickell and Son Ltd

For Ginny

If this is worth to find,
In a city's wreck or hidden
Under some lucky stone

Half the way to a hilltop,
After the holocaust,
It says, to whomsoever,

Just what it says. Someone
Was bidden to bind the wounds
The evil make, the brutal

Severings love must try
To salve: these were his only
Ways of healing, if . . .

Acknowledgments are made to *The Listener*, *The Poetry Review*, *The New Statesman*, *BBC*, *Argo* and *Jupiter* for poems already printed, broadcast or recorded.

Contents

The Weathercock

The weathercock knows each twist
And alley in the city
Of air. It knows for certain
Where nowhere is. "Go on,"
It says, "Go straight ahead.

"Never turn round and run
"With your back to Time thinking
"You can catch what you've done
"Like the blown-off hat
"Of your lost youth.

"Go where I point you, go
"Walking into the wind,
"To the source of solitude
"Where all your images
"Will blend in truth.

"Say to yourself, 'I am here, now,
"Walking into the wind,
"But the wind will change.
"I will face it, whatever quarter
"It blows from, till I'm dead.' "

Jude the Obscure to Sue Bridehead

(*Or any lover to his longed-for beloved*)

I must not know. I must.
A coin with two blank faces –
Both are yours, are mine,
Are neither both, the date
Is known, is not, is ever.

There is no common coin
No head or tail of lust
Exchangeable for this.
None knows what it is worth;
To spin it is our fate,

Whichever way it falls,
Save that it never falls –
Nor shall, till you and I
Lie in the mint of earth
And cannot care who calls.

More than Time

Loving you more than time has time for,
Not starved of earthlife, certainly not
Wanting to sing part-songs in heaven
With those we loved and, so, keep on earth;
Lying awake planning for more of
Our lives as in our time, I reach
For my luminous watch. It's stopped. How shall I
Set it? – No less a universe
Than is outside. But day will '*break*'
– A hard word for a new thing –
Then guess the time, wind up the springs
Of love, of darkness, for a start.

Away

Where am I? On what map?
What scale is there between
Another map and mine?
What life by mile or thought
Makes scales of being alone –
One thoughtless word and a thousand
Miles of a frown?

Distance; nearness; a map
Well-read can mean escape
Or the longed-for, chosen,
Impossible to have found.
Words are maps, too, of where
We maybe dont want to be
Discovered on dead ground.

Mercator was not unsound
In his projecting a flat
Fantasy of what's round,
Or seems to be – things not
As they are – equator and pole
In lines that cant be true
But serve the compromise.

All maps deceive deceivers.
Perhaps we lovers
Of 'world enough and time'
Use them only to know
Where we are not to go.
Where we are, has no scale
Of all-or-nothing. It is.

Letters

How more than alone we are
Reading or writing letters:
It means one is away
Or there's no need to write,

And like time-lag of light
From an outer star my words
May shine on your tomorrow
From my dark yesterday.

If You Feel Grievous

If you feel grievous for
A love believed in, and find
It was never, O never demand

Any giving back: it was all
Lovingly given – think
Of some ever-receiving place

Like limestone hills where grief
Sinks deep as common rain
Silently and the common

Valley is loud with streams
She could drink from, herself, alone,
A stranger, thirsty as you.

Accept

Accept: no past is
What any present was.
The secrets kept are kept,
Things must be as they are
Revealed, passed on, possessed
By those who will never know
How the wound may hurt far less
Then the scar it leaves. Accept.

I

A Roman Birth

No season, but its own
Beginning of its own
World's end; a heart belling
Universe to attend

Service in time and place:
Eyes opening, leaves turning,
Blood burning its course
Through day and night.

II

A Greek Death

Survey the sky
For that dark star
All mortals steer by.

Sometime, noon or midnight,
It will shine piercing bright,
And fall into your eye.

A Season for All Men

In spring bees pollinate
A dying-at-the-root
Or a lusty young apple-tree,
So long as it blossoms.

They do this stint by rote
For hive and queen, unwittingly
Glutting the autumn wasps
On rotten fruit.

This sort of civil service
Should lead to Higher Office –
It can for men, a winter
Letter that offers Honours

In a New Year List. One difference:
It is seldom that wasps and bees
Sting each other. Men
Pollinate as they please . . .

A Season Lost

Well then, a season lost:
So far? as if a bear
Had died in hibernation
When no seasons were?

You city-ones so lost
Without bud, brown leaf, or what
In airless rooms you are told
Will thrive in central heat –

Do you know that a lost love
Can wake too soon in spring
And savour the central cold
Of the earth's awakening?

And rejoice in a season lost
With the bears and bees and flowers
Moving so surely into
Your seasonless city hours?

The Lost Road

– "But you *must* know the lost
Road – we played there as children . . ."
She assumed we would know *their* map . . .

– A common assumption costing
Much pain: an uncommon reference
If you happen to find the way . . .

So, hope the accosted strangers
Are kindly enough not to be
Too sure where they are . . .

The clash comes at a cross-road
Signpost by nature mute
But forced to at least a half-truth.

Dead Flowers

Dry in a dusty room,
They had roots once, but now
Are grievous on graves of no-one
Seems to remember whom.

You go to chuck them out
But at the first touch feel
A deadness chill your fingers
And run to your own roots.

Night

A clear dark light: for once
You see what the universe is
As much as mortal eye can.
But sages must organise
A million million light years
To penetrate our glasses
And horrify us into being
Blind second-seeing man.

Waters

A note on Genesis Chapter I

"The Spirit of God moved
Upon the face of the waters."
Though modern Science has proved

This "week" of the Creator's
Was really millions of years,
The mystery is what matters.

We're here for better or worse
Manning this world spinning
In a crack of the Universe,

And whatever was "In the Beginning"
Water was there very early
And long before fish went finning

Or out of its hurly-burly
The Dry Land heaved and humped,
And lumpy or creepy-crawly

Creatures flopped waddled stumped
Slithered and flapped and began
To breathe, and the Air was pumped

Into lungs and finally Man
Yelled and inhaled it at birth
And lived. I'm sure I can

Skip millions of years of Earth
And History – we've got Fire
And the Animals havent, (but both

Must drink or we will expire.)
Let's think about Waters now –
Like the animals we require

For our needs, and tame: the cow,
For instance, for milk and butter
And meat to roast – just so

We have managed to tame water:
Dams for electric power;
Steam-turbine generator;

Tall, waisted, cooling-tower;
Domestic gurgling pipe,
Washing-machine and shower;

Tap (trickle and spurt and drip);
Reluctant wash, and pleasant
Splash when the bath's too deep:

Tame water's so ever-present
It's hard to think of it wild
When so obviously it isnt.

But even a glassful spilled
Spreads more than you think it could;
Water is still self-willed.

Quiet rills can rise to flood,
Rear, roll great boulders down,
Or like a blood-mad crowd

Rage house-high through a town,
Leave havoc, wreck, disaster,
Babies swept off to drown.

And remember, the Sea is your master
From the first toe you dip
As a timid toddling taster

On its smiling summer lip.
It can scupper the strongest swimmer,
Shatter the safest ship,

It is fiercer, gurlier, grimmer
Than fire with a gale to fan it,
Whether mid-sea moil, or comber

Crashing on chalk or granite
Of cliff and reef and rock,
As if to engulf the planet

And sink it whole like an Ark,
With everything living in it,
To the bottom of the dark

Back to where God began it.
You'd do well to be wise to water:
Clouds burst and hail and rain it,

Frost stills it and tempts the skater,
Springs rise, dews fall, eyes weep,
Brown muck slurps down the gutter,

Great oceans are five miles deep,
It will not flow uphill,
Both tarn and turbine keep

Its secret, its free will;
It never lets you forget
It can serve, save, and kill,

Was there first, and is wet.

Breath

So to inhale, expel,
The yeasty air, so to stay
On the empty side of the scales,

So to be how it is
To be, so to be not
How it was, and still to be

On the empty side of the scales;
So to be no-one knows,
When they burn or dig you in,

Which is the freer side
To weigh body or world in;
What has to equal what?

A Poet's Winter Song

Cold is what surely brings
  The shyest birds close
For snap of crust or crumb.
  They do not come to sing,
They have to eat as chance
  Allows, if boughs in spring
    Are to bear their season's grace,
      To sing later, later.

So cold it can be before
  We see each other closer
In a tongue-frozen anger.
– Then throw out hates and hungers,
Not waste, but sustenance:
  So eat and sing at once,
    "Now love forever now."

Composers

(for Malcolm Arnold)

Think of composers exploring
Without language but still believing
It worth not using words

To explain wherever they went to,
Or meant to – only listen
To their measurements of time

That have no morrows. Notations
Are other, exact as bills,
Remoter than the sun,

Let them borrow enough
To have time to keep going
Owing you and the gods
More or less of the earth.

Orchestra

I suppose that music critics
Must use from other arts
Words to explain composers,

– Like "colourful" "spare" "poetic"
And so on. I see two things,
The shape of an orchestra,

Its instruments, their users
And the various sorts of tadpoles
One calls a score. What then?

"The music of the spheres" –
Sound – once a conception
Of the likeliness of god.

Watching the sweating brass,
Mortal as me, I still
Hear them and see them blowing

Immortal sounds whose secrets
Unknowingly they pass
For mortal ears to keep.

What Another Thrush Said

A thrush stands on a Golden Bough
Each winter singing, "Not this way
"To under-after-worlds! I stay
"To tell you how

"To stay, as you together wake."
Then the to-come and the departed
Since we became two singlehearted
Lovers for life's sake

Seem Blake's Eternity – but made
Of what it took a thrush to be
On a Golden Bough and ask no fee
That could be owed or paid.

All Other Loved Places

Writing this, all other loved places
I would choose to be in are visible
As his angels were to Blake.
– They are just such messengers,
Mongers of values other
Than wind the clock of the world.

They proffer what no changes
Of currencies could, a loan
Of man-alive on security
Of whatever Elsewheres count,
And they bring back news of yourself
To yourself, if only you'll listen.

Lincoln Cathedral

(for Jean Rowntree)

Midnight, and twelve dark doves
Fly over the breathing city
From this colossal fabric
Fast on its spur of rock.
What measure of day begins
Within a cathedral
Where time cannot pray for man?
What evidence of love
Can the hours bring back?

Four gray doves rouse a thrush;
On every farm a cock consoles
Peter for being a human rock,
The beasts wake from their ark of night,
And all over England
There is natural hunger. Give us this day.
What measure of day begins?
Time for the flesh and the worked stone
To own what is within.

Rievaulx Abbey

June afternoon

They were there before my eyes were.
I picked with greed because
I loved them, because we first
Found them together: *Primula Farinosa*
Poised on slender austere columns,
Elegant umbels of rare wild flowers,
But as if carved, no less
Destructible than stone:
"*Leave them to seed,*" she said,
"*They live here in this valley.*"

"Renounce this world," St. Bernard
Bade his brethren, "but use your hands."
Some found gold for the virginal finger
Of this northern valley: Roman-eyed
Saw the pure site – good stone
From the dalehead; water; durable pasture.
Their strong austere columns
And slender arches grew, a stone flowering
No man would pick but for love
Of God or the Holy Virgin.

We stroll towards the altar now
No tense of time can ruin,
Our primulas in a basket
Death-delayed by a sop of moss;
The weathers of this world
Roll the abbey slowly away.
"*Leave them to seed,*" I pray,
"*The flowers, the wilting stones,*
"*They live here in this valley.*"

On Kingston Down

September 1940–1966

The harvest was good,
But from the stubble
Eying the Channel
Some thought of the yield in France,
But hardly of bread there;

Eying the vapour-trails
Coiled in the sky passes,
Like vast demented ploughings,
They mapped last-seeming acres
For our reaping.

The yield was late but good.
There was a grain that made
More than daily bread.
Children now, hardly knowing
They know its savour,

Eat it this calm evening;
And in the stubble,
Now as then,
Heartsease in late flower –
A grace unspoken.

A Postcard from Eskdale

I

The sun pours over the dale
Hue after hue of light,
None fixed but each one true.

What is the quintessence?
We punctuate a place
Older than any words

And hard to pick a bone
Of living from, hard indeed
To dig and bury one's bones;

Not hard to die in.
While we touched, the sun was fingering,
As indifferently as seed

On stone, two climbers' bodies
That all this copious day
Were splayed beneath a crag.

While seeming safe together
We posted the broad view
With our love to death, so lightly,

They lay with stagnant blood
As if water lay still,
Dead, at its fall's foot.

II

Inquest and definition,
Moment and infinite meaning,
Things of their nature sought

Always too late. What did I say?
Could you not hear for the beat
Of the stone heart in the sinews

Of the splayed immutable water?
For the air's avowals? The sun's
Explications of cloud and clear?

Three words no man no woman
On earth can hear too often
Or twice the same. *I love you.*

You must hear them beside me, and there –
At the cold crag foot
Where the stones hold no echoes.

The sun pours over the dale
Hue after hue of light,
None fixed but each one true.

Coming down the Fell

What chance made the stream
Take a new course? Only
Ten yards away I could hear
The water at its needful
Incantations that shake
Stones in their deaf dream
To wake and seem to hop
Like frogs or podded seeds;
Only ten yards away
In its new bed the water,
Loving insomniac,
Was wheedling every stone
Into not saying "stop" to it.

But here there were still dry stones,
A skeleton of violence,
Evidence but no clue
Of violence old or new:
A rock-fall after storm
Like heart-break, or the slow
Nibbling of mouse-drops
On a flawed rock, like doubt
Or jealousy; but somehow
The course was changed and ate
The soil over the hump,
A mere ten yards to the left.
I stopped and drank my fill there.
But it is still my thirst
I remember most, clambering
Over the dry bed.

Some hour of rain the fell
May shrug and shift again,

And every blind stone weep
For joy, and thank the waters
For giving them back the reflection
Of skies they used to keep.

Sputnik

Before I saw my first
Sputnik I'd seen, that morning,
Two very old men repairing
A bit of dry-stone wall
In a dalehead lane whose signpost
Said: "Impassable for motors."

Not stopping, levering more
Than a man's weight, one said
"Last night, did you see that sputnik?"
And went on working. My child
Stayed up as it grew dark
To see "a shooting star".

He shrugged the sputnik off
In boredom as it flared by
And went to bed frustrated.
It was my luck to see
"A shooting star" not long
After the sputnik passed.

I thought as I saw the meteor
Burn out in our atmosphere
Of my child's world asleep
And of those two old craftsmen.
I had no grandiose thoughts
Of ten thousand technologists,

But pondered as I saw
The regimen of air
Invaded so, and looked
At the pole star and the wall
And wished for a world so steered
Levered back repaired
For a child to wake in safe.

St. Catherine's Point

Here now. Five hundred feet
High on the granite point.
Three ways to look: inland
From the cliff-edge, a plough
Tows its kite-tail of gulls.
Above, pure blue. No cloud.
We stand in a shell of brightness
As if this field when fledged
With its corn would fly us upward
In a song as pre-ordained
As a lark in the sun's eye.
Here now. In warmth and light:
The sky save for its birds
Naked, untenanted.

The clouds have fallen, fallen,
They lie on the sea below us.
Here now. Hundreds of miles
Of cold candescent vapour.
Fifty feet high, but within it
Ships move in a sweat of fear,
A grind of groping, calling
Where are you?
                    We seem to stand
High on this granite point
At ease in the clear light,
Everything clear, the ploughshare
Its glittering frozen wave
Breaking the brown earth,
The life so surely planted . . .

Where are we? Where is here?

The Quarrel

A cantata for the 800th centenary of St. Thomas Becket. Music composed by Alan Ridout. First performance, Canterbury Cathedral, July 18th 1970.

Note: the two verses of the Anthem are taken from an Anonymous early 14th century hymn.

I

Anthem

Plaude Cantuaria
  plausu renovato,
laude multifaria
  Deum collaudato,
urbs sanctificata,
firmiter fundata,
Deo consecrata,
  pretioso sanguine
praesulis ornata,
  et sancti solamine
Thomae solidata.

II

The Time 1154 et sqq.

From the coming of Norman William
  Hardly a hundred years;
England a land of turmoil
  Ravaged by petty wars,

Baron besieges Baron,
  Rules at his own will;
One law for the rich, none for the poor;
  Trial by ordeal still.

Young Henry loves feasting
  And feminine delights:
Sets a sober Chancellor
  To put his realm to rights.

Becket orders his kingdom,
  Rebuilds great London Tower;
Abbot and Baron have to bow
  Before his temporal power.

III

Character of King Henry

Absolute Monarch
Not to be crossed,
Yet his passion is
For justice.
A piercing mind
Fuddled by rage
Yet to his age
Gives justice.

Fooling in Mass
His cold mind plans
To make the Church
His slave of State,
Becket his tool.
Pride cannot brook
As prior claim
God before Crown.

Vision can turn
To blinding hate,
His thwarted mind
Can murder.
Yet when the blood
Clears from his head
He still fosters law
And order.

IV

Character of Thomas Becket

Who is Becket – one man? Who is Thomas – another?
In his splendour a king; in his cup at the feast
There is water. In the midst of the Court, uncorrupt.
Debonair but devout, quick to act but a lawyer,
Without self in his work for the Crown and aware
Of the power and the glory; but the servant of God.

Who is Thomas – one man? Who is Becket – another?
As he gave to the King he shall give to the Church.
He is single in passionate zeal: neither play,
Neither part, is for him to decide – he must act,
And be stubborn for God beyond pride or humility.
From the double of flesh he will tear the same spirit.

V

The Quarrel

Choir: Justice! Church or King's Law?
Principles! Becket stubborn,
Now yielding, now recanting,
Claiming his oath unlawful.

Henry (recit): Two-faced traitor! Swearing obedience "in word of truth" but "saving your order" "saving God's honour" – swearing to anything, meaning nothing!

Choir: Hatred stains the quarrel.
Henry, Becket's master,
Shall have his servant humbled,
Or who is England's ruler?

Henry (recit): Low-born clerk, who set you up in pride of place? It was my will, my will! What gratitude to your King? As I made you, Thomas Becket, so shall I break you!

Choir: King's Court, Barons, Bishops –
Becket on temporal charges –
Free in his power as Prelate
Flouts them, refusing trial.

Beckett (recit): God's Will be done, I submit to no Will but His. I did not choose my office. I was freely given to God. No man shall dare oppose Him. Let the King give me at Mass the kiss of peace. God's Will be done!

Choir: Who is England's ruler?
Thomas murdered martyr?
Or Royal Henry kneeling
Scourged before God's altar?

VI

The King and the Knights

"O King, while yet this Thomas lives,
 "No peace nor quiet can be!"
"Traitor! Low-born clerk!" The King
 Cursed in a black fury.

They read on his brow, they read in his eye,
 They read in his writhing lip
The sign of death. Up leapt four knights
 Headlong to horse and ship.

"Meet we at Saltwood Castle!"
 Their rowels rained with blood.
Four roads they galloped, four ships they took,
 Till each in England stood.

Morville, Brito, FitzUrse, de Traci
 Never drew rein nor breath
Till they met at Saltwood Castle
 To vow again one death.

VII

The Murder

The Choir is split up.

They are coming . . .
Listen, an axe . . .
Fly, fly my lord . . .
An axe at the door . . .
No safety here . . .
Into the Church . . .

(*In the Church, Vespers is being sung*)

Bolt the door . . .
Darkness darkness . . .
To the roof – crypt – roof . . .
Christ save us . . .
Bolt the door . . .

God's Church is no fortress
Let the door be!
Crypt – roof – Blood of Christ! . . .
To the altar . . . save us . . .
They are coming!

Hither, King's men!
Where is the traitor?

No traitor but Priest of God!
What do you want?

Priest of treachery!
Tear his tongue out!
Split his skull!
Quarter his guts!

What do you want?

Your death – death – DEATH!
I submit to death –
Come out, prisoner!
I shall not move –
Seize him! . . . drag him! . . .
Off! off! Take off your hands! . . .
You are a dead man . . . dead . . . dead!
Then do your work!
Death to the traitor!
(strikes) de Traci!
Into Thy hands
(strikes) FitzUrse!
I commend
(strikes) Brito!
My spirit
(strikes) Morville!

Each knight utters his name with a savage yell. Behind the words "Death to the traitor!" form a continuous pattern, and after the climax of the fourth knight diminish into silence on a final "Death . . ."

VIII

Repentance of the King: Grief of the people

Alto: Thomas forgive me, dear earliest counsellor!
Choir: Thomas our shepherd, protector, O lost to us!
Alto: Lost to me, blinded, my hatred was all to me!
Choir: To all of us thirsting our fountain of holiness!

Alto: Father in God, believe in my innocence!
Choir: Innocence murdered, O horrible sacrilege!
Alto: Evil my thoughts, never mine their embodiment!
Choir: None can restore our beloved Archbishop!

Alto: Thomas, too late I cry out in my agony!
Choir: Blessèd his agony, cursèd his murderers!
Alto: Never your murderer, grant me my innocence!
Choir: Pray for the soul of Saint Thomas of Canterbury!

IX

Anthem

Salve, lux laetitiae,
lumen confessorum,
Thoma, sol ecclesiae,
solamen Anglorum:
tu justi juvamen,
tu maestis solamen,
tu lapsis levamen,
tu nostra memoria,
nostrum medicamen,
tibi laus et gloria,
virtus, honor. Amen.